# VITAL SIGNS

# Vital Signs

*Poems*

## ROSS WILSON

RED SQUIRREL PRESS

First published in 2023 by Red Squirrel Press
36 Elphinstone Crescent
Biggar
South Lanarkshire
ML12 6GU
www.redsquirrelpress.com

Edited by Colin Will

Layout, design and typesetting by Gerry Cambridge
e: gerry.cambridge @btinternet.com

Cover graphic: Milagli/Shutterstock.com

A CIP catalogue record for this book is available from
the British Library.

ISBN: 978 1 913632 39 7

Red Squirrel Press is committed to a sustainable future.
This publication is printed in the UK by Imprint Digital
Using Forest Stewardship Council certified paper.
www.digital.imprint.co.uk

## TO AMANDA

*I looked into my palms*
*as staff cleaned blood from*
*the bed you'd been on,*
*my hands locking in some*

*anxious atheist prayer*
*as a new voice pierced the air*
*loud and clear and healthy*
*as I hoped you were.*

*Because you were and are,*
*and because we're here,*
*my ragged script scrawls*
*a zig-zag across paper*

*like vital signs that spell:*
*we are,*
      *we are,*
           *we are.*

CONTENTS

I. *Arrivals & Departures*

II. *Days & Nights*

# I

# Arrivals & Departures

# A SHORT WALK

The maternity ward is a short walk
from the ICU where I work
long shifts among lives in the balance
and visitors counting the breaths
of those unable to breathe for themselves.

As I walked out on my break one day
I thought of the rooms I cleaned
in hotels when I was young;
the arrivals and departures, the bus tours,
the never-ending revolving doors.

My reflection moved in a window
framing the Necropolis beyond its pane.
Then the atmosphere changed like a season;
the cold winter air I'd been breathing in
turned warm as spring in bloom.

A tiny finger curled my thumb.
I cradled a bundle of flesh and bone.
Where did she come from?
The obvious answer couldn't explain
the lightness in my arms.

Or the heaviness in my head
as I returned to work, carrying
the weight of what I know:
the maternity ward is a short walk
from a long shift in ICU.

## JOCK TAMSON'S TAXI

The driver's face was a lump of dough
kneaded by events and people.
Or so I imagined as he waddled
towards me. Fat wobbled
under an XXL shirt.
Sweat oozed a rancid odour.
Cynicism seeped from every pore.
To sit beside him in a car
was to be in a room where
the bulb has blown.

Yet, when I mentioned you, born
the day before, something in him
switched on.
Whatever he'd become,
whatever the years had beaten into him
was forgotten in the moment when
he beamed with joy for a wean
he'll never know.
To think, even this crabbit auld man
was somebody's bairn.

## SHINE

The year you took centre stage in our lives
was the best summer anyone could remember.
The sun blazed a spotlight over your pram
as we wheeled you through Roukenglen.

You'd peer up at those big yins
who'd reach for you with arms
like branches that stretched over their heads
so shadow-bars alternated with blinding rays.

New sensations blurred in a brain where
a million neural connections sparked per second
under a wee hat you loved to rip off
as if its tight grip restricted your growth.

Data streamed in; *Da-da* flowed out
in a gaze fixed on me, in days when memory
was short and quickly eclipsed
like the sun you won't remember.

I catch what I can with my pen
so that when you read this poem
the light that graced you as a bairn
will shine in you again.

## JOY

You'd haul yourself up
on my leather foot-stool
and sway, thumping
a chubby fist like a gavel,
erupting baby babble.

The stool's slanted angle
made an ideal lectern
for a mini-preacher
pontificating in her pulpit.
Fluffy toys along the couch

were your assembly.
With no words to say
you preached word-sounds,
*a-ga! a-da! da-da-da!*
in a sermon on pure joy.

## DUET

Before you could talk
you'd fingerpick a lip
like a guitarist playing chords.

Later, when your vocal cords
picked words from babble
you'd shout *Bubbles!*

from a bath-full, or yell
*books,* toddling towards a box
to pull one from the pile.

Then, flicking pages together,
our fingers conducted images
from silent scores of paper.

## LIKENESSES

Thumb over thumb
I create wings that flap
towards our daughter
giggling in her high chair.
She watches fingers soar
over a muted tv
where images show
what happens when
a man's hands release
what's in them
from one land to another,
across oceans.

As I cross the room,
my dove-shaped hands
become a cup
scooping our baby up
like the arms of a man
carrying the dangling limbs
of a child on the tv
beside me,
out of sound,
if not quite out of sight,
our likenesses
reflected in its light.

## DEAD MAN'S FALL

When playing Dead Man's Fall
we'd stand atop a wall and call
*Grenade! Bazooka! Pistol!*

Then, after a dramatic leap,
our limbs would star-shape
the grass, or crash in a heap.

At forty-one I jumped from
a climbing frame
to impress a girl, almost three.

No damage done, an alarm
shrieked from knees
that cracked like rams'

skulls, battering the meaning
of pain and mortality
into the brain, via the body.

SKELF

Watching our three-year-old ascend
a rope ladder on a climbing frame
I started to run, afraid she'd fall
from the top rung, when her arms
pulled her up onto the platform
and the ladder swung

from her sole into me,
three decades before, grappling,
gripping trunk and branch,
and pulling myself up out of reach
of the big boys I'd provoked
into chasing me up a tree

I'd loaded with divots;
turf-bombs perched like birds
to bombard my pursuers before
I leaped tree-to-tree, and down
upon garage roofs, away from
big angry feet clacking after me.

Ticking hands grabbed me
in the moment our girl splashed
grey into my hair in a dash
of daring, a stubborn ladder tread,
agile as the young-lad self
buried in her Dad like a skelf.

# THE EYE OF A NEEDLE

'Very imaginative content.
Spelling needs attention.'
—Mrs Taplin, 19th May 1989,
Kelty Primary School Report.

My first lesson in irony
was Mrs Woods calling me
*The Sewing Champion.*
I was far more interested in
sowing my imagination
onto the blank page.
All through primary school
my mind moved slow
as a car on a road full
of dunce-cap cones.
Spelling and grammar went
over a head deep under
dreams of its own making.
I'd divide a page in my jotter
and draw cartoon characters
on either side, figures like
The Ochs and The Hoochs;
wee tartan-clad clans
in a never-ending war.
The Ochs, crabbit, in a huff,
oching, harrumphing, reaching
for claymores and shotguns
as the Hoochs' ceilidh
kicked-off over the page.
Across the classroom
some teacher would be
blethering on and on
as my pen pressed in to paper
like a needle.

## MASTER KEY

*Personal care? Oh, I couldn't do that!*
People tell me, squirming at the thought.
But what a great feeling
leaving a vulnerable person
better off than when you found them.

*You must be a poof,* real men
have said to me, as if compassion
had anything to do with sexuality.
Even the best intentions miss wildly:
think of *angel* or *hero* on *Thank You* cards.

The first time I really hurt someone
he parried my jabs, slipped my crosses,
so I threw an uppercut:
he staggered across the ring.
Killer instinct kicked in—

I sensed blood before I saw it.
The word *key* is masculine in German,
feminine in Spanish.
It's surprising what we have inside us
when we need to unlock it.

## GRIFFITH

> 'I kill a man and most forgive me...
> I love a man and many say this makes
> me an evil person.'
> —Emile Griffith

Emile Griffith weighed light as a fairy
according to a grinning Benny Paret.
To be gay in 1962 was to be mentally ill
according to the American Psychiatric Association.
The *New York Times* would not print 'homosexual'.
'Un-man' was their alternative label
for a human being so able in a boxing ring
he couldn't be boxed in by anything
so simple as a stereotype.

A milliner before he was a boxer.
The press called Griffith *The Mad Hatter
of Manhattan*. Paret called him a *maricon*.
At a time when most conformed
to rigid roles as men and women,
masculine and feminine were one in him.
Griffith loved designing women's hats
and hit Paret so hard and often
he died.

# THE UPSIDE-DOON TREE

*i.m. Billy Hunter*

> 'Everybody does not see alike. To the eyes of a miser a guinea is
> far more beautiful than the Sun, and a bag worn with the use of
> money has more beautiful proportions than a vine filled with
> grapes. The tree which moves some to tears of joy is in the Eyes of
> others only a Green thing that stands in the way.'
> —William Blake, Letter to Revd. Dr. Trusler, 1799

*That tree looks upside-doon,* you said
and it did. I only saw what you saw
from the couch of my parents' house
because you'd invited yourself
after I let slip they were on holiday.
You bought a crate of beer for me to lug:
they didn't call you Billy Bud
because you read Melville,
though one time you did ask to hear
some of my writing and I recited
around 4am in some flat stinking
of hash and cigarettes and alcohol
the opening paragraph of a novel
revision had beaten into my brain.
Pissing my dole money down the drain,
I heard your too-loud voice boom:
*Ross is a guid cunt.*

Michelangelo liberated sleeping spirits
from stone: I fumbled to tell of a poison
locking men in skulls like prison.
Back then I was drifting into poetry
as you, more than a decade older,
were going downhill. You told me
one time laughing in your telling
of your walk home down a brae

stumbling from the pub into a jog.
I still hear your baritone *ho-ho-ho*
though don't like to think of you
slumped where you were found. No,
I see you as the upside-doon tree
upended in a storm, roots ripped
from where you might settle or grow,
a guid cunt whose boots tripped
on the way home.

# THE SLEEPING GIANT

*—i.m. Ramsay Mackay, 1945–2018*

> I'm the witchdoctor of Hillbrow
> And I can sleep just like the dead
> Though I will always live forever
> —Ramsay Mackay


There can't have been many who knew
The Zulu Dance of Death in Kelty.
Ramsay Mackay did.
He didn't just know it: he did it in the pub.
A big man with a Walt Whitman beard,
Ramsay looked like he'd blown in
from the nineteenth century
via the sixties counterculture.

Everyone was Ramsay's brother.
When someone objected, 'Ah'm no yir brithir,'
he was corrected, 'We're all brothers, brother.'
Introduced to 'Ramsay, the Poet,'
I must have been a midge around his beer,
nipping his head about Rimbaud and Baudelaire.
A legendary bass player and singer,
I'd no idea how much he'd done.

Years later, YouTubing his name,
I came upon song after song after song
scrawled by his hand, sung in his unique
Scots-born, South African tongue.
Ramsay carried a notebook like a wallet.
It had no market value, but
if words were gold, Ramsay was rich.
'He lives up Benarty,' I was told.

The Sleeping Giant, to locals,
Benarty hill's outline against the skyline
is a Gulliver tied down in Lilliput.
I remember Ramsay, well over six foot,
kicking snow off his boots
in a bar where joints were rolled on tables.
Back then I kept my interest in literature
so close to my chest it made an impression.

Ramsay blew in like permission
to be myself. A gentleman, his individualism
didn't conflict with the community:
he stood out and blended in—
a sore thumb, warm in the village glove.
Though he sleeps now like the dead
when you press *play* he wakes
and makes a dance of life out of death.

## BRETT'S JUKEBOX KITCHEN
(a cookery/poetry/music TV show)

*—For Brett Evans*

You can't smell through the screen
but you can tell the air is full of spices
as you feel your toes tapping
to the pre-war rural blues Brett has spun
on the juke. And you can see the big man
himself pouring another gin by the laptop
set up beside the toaster. And you can hear
him cursing the latest poet wanker
blind as Milton when it comes
to reading submission guidelines.
*Blind also, because he's a wanker,*
*dear viewer,* Brett tells the camera,
making a gesture with his hand
and turning from the laptop
to a chopping board. *Let's pretend*
*this onion is a poet's head.*
Brett guillotines with relish.
*Viewers! You must guess the dish*
*of the day from the clues my juke*
*blows into the air like Little Walter*
*bending notes. Yes, we're digging up*
*ingredients buried in the airwaves*
*of the Twenties, The Roaring Twenties,*
*not the Coughing-Covid-Tweeting-Twenties.*
*THEY can fuck right off!*
Brett jabs the juke and Bessie Smith
pours into 2021 like a jug full of cream.
*To poetry, music, good food!*
Brett announces, raising his gin.
*Chin-chin!*

## GERRY'S NEST

*—For Gerry Cambridge*

Pens pocketed on his breast
like chicks in a nest,
beak-tips loaded with words
like the songs of birds.

## A PINCH OF SNUFF

Twenty years ago I looked at him
in the back of a van driving home
from a factory. He was telling me
about his bleeding ulcers.

The motion shook his lager can
as froth foamed a walrus tache
and a window framed hair
like a kicked-in nest.

Twenty years later, he peered up
over snuff heaped on the back
of a hand bony and veined
as the roots of a tree.

*Yir hame! Hoo ye gittin oan, son?*
We only spoke in passing;
the moment, a pinch of snuff,
there, then gone, into the head.

## x28

The X28 flows upstream
like a salmon swallowing minnows.
I'm one. It sucks me in
and moves on through the rain
in the early morning dark.

A man's yawn spreads like a virus
down through the bus;
a woman scrolls her phone;
a man skims the *Metro*.
Glasgow looms in the windscreen.

It's 06:40 am.
My day's light will be eaten
by a twelve-hour shift.
Better eaten than wasted.
Better absorbed into life

than let rot like the road-kill
I glimpse on the M80;
a bloody pulp of gristle and fur
too far among the turning wheels
to re-enter the circle.

I feed hours to work
so I can feed my family,
the x on the destination screen
a box ticked, a vote counted,
not a day scored out.

# DEAD WOMAN'S HAND

*17 April, 2013*

The day of her funeral
nurses moved from woman
to woman, their hands full
of bedpans and basins while
politicians droned on and on
about her.

Eulogies fouled the air
in an auld hospital tower,
posh voices wafting among
stools and urine into the ears
of women who were alert,
if eerily quiet.

Then something said jarred
and a broad Fife brogue
brushed the air blue
like a cue for others to chip in.
All but one who
kept her opinion

tucked under blanket and sheet,
discreet as the hand
of a card player in a game
that was far from over,
though some began to cheer
as if they'd won a war.

## COMRADE

A Tory and a Royalist, Tam
was always welcome in the mining club
among men who saw him as a man
then a daft bastard, but only then.
For if Tam voted against the interests of his own
it wasn't because he was mean.

He'd have done anything for anyone
and never viewed a human being as vermin
unlike some champions of Socialism
who'd turn dictator in their own home;
women and bairns cowed to the God, Dad.
Tory, Royalist, not the brightest,

Tam was one of the best.
They called him Comrade.

# BANTER

Though I flitted a mere hour along the road,
my *twang* is commented upon,
and where I'm from becomes a game.
One thing's for sure: Ah'm no fae here!
*Yir a Teuchter,* they explain.
Sometimes I tell them, poker-faced,
*Ah'm fae Brigadoon.*

It's mostly banter, though I remember
standing in Argyle Street, looking up
at the Heilanman's Umbrella
while the Orange Order,
like some ghost-army marching
through centuries of streets,
blew new breath into auld flutes.

About me, newsstands headlined
the latest refugee crisis;
above, the Umbrella: a rail bridge where
people sheltered together;
around, distant drums beat a grim reminder—
how quickly banter can turn;
how easily We become *Us* and *Them.*

DEEF

*Classical music is elitist,*
Jimmy insisted.
You'd never see Jimmy
listening to that
upper-class shite.

*Class-ical; class-ical,*
he'd say, emphasizing class
as if the word hung
above him like some
cold superior icicle.

Jimmy liked his music
doon tae earth
so his feet could tap
the grund, at one
with the beat under his feet.

One day, his grandson
told him about the time
Beethoven turned his back on
an aristocrat passing
in a carriage.

Next time he saw the bairn
Jimmy was overwhelmed.
*The 9th! The 9th!*
*Fucking hell son!*
*Naebdy telt mae aboot the 9th!*

## THE WHYS

For the stranger who found him
hung from a tree, the why
didn't enter until well after
the shock of discovery
and the attempted resuscitation.
Sleepless with that young face
frozen in his head, the why
became an obsession.

For the mother the why was there
from the start, less a thought
than a refrain, *Why? Why? Why?*
spurting from a mouth open as a wound.
Later, the whys couldn't get out;
like wasps trapped in a bag,
a buzzing panic, the *why sons?*
became constant stings.

For the mother of his child
the whys had an answer.
Friends reassured her: no-one
would resort to *that* for what she done;
more had to be going on.
And maybe there had been, but her why
was also a guilty *because*, mixed with anger:
*why abandon our daughter?*

For the best friend who, two decades before,
shared a sandpit with him, sieving
gold grains into a bucket
(no concept of time, just fun)
the why was locked in
fists clenched so tight nails broke skin,
though jacket pockets buried them
from eyes watching.

For the nurse who bagged him
the why was disturbing.
For this was no cancer-ridden auld man
but a healthy handsome fit one
*my own age.* It felt wrong taping a sheet
over a face with decades left to run.
But his years ran out
in the minutes a rope spun.

## REMEMBRANCE SERVICE, 1936

You stand head and shoulders
above the crowd at the Soldier,
reflecting on the names of the fallen,
contemplating the Great War before
the second one yet to happen.

The mine he hated will save your son,
reigning him in from the war to come,
and making possible a hand that writes
some ninety years after this photo's frame
opened a window in time as the light

soles of your Great-Great-Granddaughter,
weeks on her feet, enter the room to her
shouting, *Dada Dada Dada!* I turn
from a yellow press clipping and gather
a bundle of giggles as the seconds run.

# HOPE STREET, 2017

The bus stop framed in this pub window
reminds me of a story I wrote years ago.
'Where Ye Gaun?' was the title.
I see Hope Street glow on a bus timetable
through my reflection ghosting the pane.
Election posters are plastered on
buses like alternative destination screens
promising people places they can be taken
if they let themselves be taken in.

A nonentity celebrity never-was
has been blown out of all proportion:
a selfie God with no talent or skill;
a perpetual teenager who can't even pull
a smile from the face Reality TV bought him.
The bus his image is on passes
as I turn to faces framed by the gantries.
I scroll down my newsfeed:
friends are un-friending, blocking, deleting.

People can't see the shape-shifter truth
morphing into whatever they can see
from wherever they happen to be.
Online debates explode and spread wildfire.
I see a poster on a bus featuring a man
like a Pied Piper leading immigrants to the shore.
To some, it's a postcard from the Third Reich.
To others, a ticket home to a country
they no longer feel is their own.

I sit in Scotland, in the Divided Kingdom,
on the edge of Europe, scrolling for a golden mean
among slogans and memes and Tricksters
convincing others of The Truth.

Those who can't see it will be deleted
so those who do can tell each other
what they already know.
Voices echo in the chamber in my palm.
I turn it off, reach for a book, open

to the flyting of MacDiarmid and Henderson:
the Scottish Literary Renaissance v.
the Folk Revival; literary culture v.
the oral tradition; page v. stage.
I absorb auld words and beer
and in my head hear an auld troubadour
sing about poets fighting in a captain's tower
while everybody is shouting
*which side are you on?*

Court jesters on opposite sides of an ocean
are competing with politicians to be king
while Mayhem darkens like a storm.
In Hope Street, traffic flows left and right
through my reflection in the pane.
My face blurs with an actor promoting a film.
I can't see much through this small frame.
I can't look out without looking in.
Which side are you on? Where we gaun?

# JANUARY MORNING, 2020

'Oh, I adore Mrs Thatcher.'
—Philip Larkin, 1979

'A bitter constituent of Larkin's disillusionment was the fact that
financial cutbacks by his beloved Mrs Thatcher had begun to haunt
Hull with the spectre of terminal decline: "I began my library career
singlehanded, and it looks as if I shall end it that way, sitting at
the turnstiles of a vast bat-haunted cobwebbed building beside one
flickering candle stuck in a bottle."'
                                        —Dennis O'Driscoll, 1996

'Libraries gave us power'
                              —Nicky Wire, *Design for Life*, 1996

'The NHS was created at a time of great austerity (much more severe
than that which the bankers and their neoliberal friends have inflicted
on the people of this country) and belongs to an era in which each of
us recognizes that we share the vulnerability of all. We must not allow
this jewel in the crown of the welfare state to be destroyed by those
whose rapacious self-interest has rendered them unable to comprehend
any notion of the public good or public service. If the corporate raiders
succeed, some of us will die from lack of care, many more will undergo
unnecessary suffering due to ill health, and more still will experience
financial ruin. This seems a high price to pay for making the world
pleasing to hedge fund managers and multinational companies, whose
interests are increasingly dominant in the corrupted parliamentary
processes shaping every aspect of our lives.'
—Raymond Tallis, NHS SOS (How the NHS was betrayed—
            and how we can save it, 2013).

>       At a bus stop in Condorrat at 6:40 am
>       I see my reflection in a graffitied shelter
>       and think how the General Election before
>       Christmas brought a gift most of us
>       could do without. It's the bicentenary year
>       of the execution of John Baird.

A former soldier, a weaver by trade,
Baird marched militants against the government
in a time when working men and women
didn't have the right to vote.
Hanged and beheaded a traitor,
resurrected a martyr centuries later,
here, in his hometown, a street and school
are named after Baird.
I board a bus that makes progress
(oh, the irony!) along a ring road circling a house
occupying the space where he once lived,
a stone's throw from the library.
Once upon a time weavers were
the most literate workers in the country.
Now weaving is history and austerity
cuts see libraries shut like unread books.

The bus is packed. Hand grips sway
like nooses on gallows above a rack of *Metro*s
stacked like some satirical magazine.
The cover frames Trump and Johnson—
the Laurel and Hardy of the fine mess we're in;
caricatures for leaders who happen
to be real as the hands on the wheel
steering us out of Condorrat into Mollinsburn,
down a slip-road and onto
the M80, accelerating to Glasgow.
I have coffee and enough food to fuel me
through a twelve-hour shift.
A badge on my uniform has the acronym,
NHS. I think of Bevan, a miner
with a major brain fed on library books
until it had grown into a position
to face the opposition and tell them:
*no society can call itself civilized if a sick person*
*is denied medical aid because of lack of means.*

The idea there's no such thing as society
became popular while I was a bairn,
drenching a generation like a corrosive rain,
eating into the seams of communities
until they burst into division and blame.
I think of Bevan and the NHS and how some
progress is possible, though steps back inevitable.
And I recall Billy Connolly quipping,
*Doctors in America have tills on their desks.*
There's profit to be made from people's pain,
and opportunists will dig in and undermine
the idea of socialized medicine,
like pickpockets dipping one hand
as they greet you with the other.
Days ago, I read about a prison in West Virginia,
contracted to a private company
providing free tablets to inmates,
then charging them five cents per minute
to rent books it would be cheaper to buy.

We go by Robroyston where Menteith
betrayed Wallace. Both
were seen by some as traitors in their time,
though Wallace, like Baird, is now a martyr.
Time can flip a reputation like a coin.
I reach for my phone. An article claims
Britain would have remained in the EU
were its population better educated.
My finger scrolls to young students
mocking Brexit Bulldog stereotypes.
They focus on bald-headed beer-bloated
angry middle-aged men with flags in fists
punching air like Union Jack-in-a-boxes.
One has a tattoo MADE IN ENGLAND
circling his belly button like a birth mark.
I imagine those words sucked down that drain

when the plug's pulled at the end of this month
and the pint of bitter he bought fills his mouth.
Fool is too tame a word for some:
they label the Brexiteers fascists,
whether they are, or far from.

Another article calls the far left an urban
cosmopolitan puritan clique and blames
the 'Corbyn cult' for losing the election.
What would auld autodidacts like Bevan
make of the 'woke' and their jargon?
And what would they make of him?
Yet another privileged cis white male?
Gammon, if his ideas don't toe the line?
Bevan was of his time, like us all.
Sometimes, at soft play, with my
two-year-old daughter I imagine
the toddlers conspiring in their giggling
to overthrow the millennials and judge them
for how wrong they were
about this and that and everything.
Time is its own revolution.
All generations are overturned;
auld-fashioned ideas condemned.
But fashions, like seasons, return.
I remember a man I knew blurting,
*Enoch Powell had the right idea.*
And I remember surprising myself
as much as him, by snapping
in an angry tone like a bark.
I can still see the look of shock
as my response slapped the smirk
from his face. Reading didn't teach me
to conform but to poke my pen in,
a Doubting Tam, fingering a wound.
I smell coffee from my flask, see hats on

heads over phones, headphones in
pumping news and music and cage fights
into brains. One is reading a book.
A book! It's open on her lap like a relic.
Is it an offensive book, I wonder?
Offensive, to who? Is it approved?
Approved of by who? My newsfeed
informs me people are cancelling books
and writers who don't fit the wee box
ideologues have pushed into their ears.
Meanwhile, a rumour of a virus in Wuhan,
a whisper a month ago, has gone up in volume.
I scroll on as the bus rolls on
through the dark. A notification:
Holocaust Remembrance Day is this week.
I recall *The Grey Zone* where Primo Levi
wrote how the young dislike ambiguity.
My greying hair makes its own zone
against the windowpane;
barbed wire tangled in the remains
of dark strands like jagged thoughts
snagging and tugging at certainty.
Glasgow appears in the reflection
of a haggard middle-aged man.
Where the hell did he come from?
How did *he* get into *my* face?
Eyes blackened from day- and night-shifts
alternating like left jabs and right crosses.
There are responsibilities ye cannae duck.
I look knackered as an auld has-been boxer
retired on his stool. A bell rings.
BUS STOPPING lights up a sign.
Instinct jolts me into action.
Slinging my bag on my back I move on
into the darkness of early morning Glasgow,
across the road, to the Royal Infirmary.

Inside, I pass a large framed portrait of a man:
  JAMES M^CCUNE SMITH.
Born a slave in Manhattan in 1813,
denied admission to medical college
due to the colour of his skin,
funds were raised for him to study in
Glasgow. Graduating top of his class,
he worked for a time at the infirmary
that stood before the one I walk through now.
The first African-American to hold a medical degree,
I imagine him walking triumphantly
through a city made rich from the slave trade
before returning to the States to work as a doctor
and a writer, fighting for abolition:
a great mind trained in statistics,
McCune Smith beat racist theories with facts.

As I enter the link corridor
connecting the auld Royal with the new,
I consider how staff are trained
to look for signs of human trafficking.
It's 2020 and signs of poverty are everywhere.
I imagine Baird a decade before
McCune Smith, marching weavers
from looms to guns to war,
and how we're all swept up in a link corridor
where the past clashes with the present
and staggers into the future;
a never-ending stream each generation
is caught in; a place where rapids
of our own making cut
between the ground we have in common.
I turn a bend into the Queen Elizabeth building,
picturing the world back when
Glasgow was the second city of the Empire
and one of the most impoverished;
a place where money poured up, rather than in.

And I think of all the poverty I've seen
alive and well in bodies so unwell;
brains battered by fists and drugs and alcohol;
a footprint on a man's face like Orwell's
prophetic metaphor stamping forever
in a stampede of greed where
the fallen are trampled in a race for profits
in the face of CUTS CUTS CUTS.
A place where libraries are shut
like minds while business rolls on,
a big bus sucking people in
and spitting them out
and running over everything in its way
as it runs on and away,
and round and round
History's not-so-merry-go-round.

# II

# Days & Nights

'I remember being told about a nurse opening a window to
release the soul of a patient who had just died and a doctor
sneering that was a lot of superstitious rubbish. Perhaps
poetry is like that window in a way? For all our wonderful
advances in technology and science and the essential need to
keep our bodies working, none of that helps us emotionally
or spiritually or however you want to word it. Poetry can be a
window into what's going on inside us. And, of course, some
will always dismiss that as rubbish while others will keep
reaching for the window.'

An excerpt from my contribution to 'The Conversation: Poets
of the NHS', published in *Gutter* magazine, Feb 2021. The
interview, conducted by Dr Colin Begg, took place between
late November and early December 2020, prior to the second
wave of Covid-19. The total number of UK deaths from Covid
on the date of publication was 129,498.

*The dark come-in!*
*The dark come-in!*

*The bairn announced*
*like a prophet seeing*

*what we were falling into*
*before it filled our window.*

## ADMISSION

Wheeled down a corridor
with a mask over nose and mouth
and finger snared by a sats probe
and ECG leads like tentacles
attached to sticky dots
sending signals to a screen
monitoring what's going on
in the body you've been
driving around for fifty years
like a car you thought had decades
left to run. Now unsure
you look up at what you can see
of faces looking down through PPE
and feel yourself whisked from
trolley to bed on a flat board
and are reassured
by mask-muffled words
of staff in goggles like bulging eyes.
Giant insects work as a team,
assembling equipment, turning
this body that's broken down
with you strapped in it
trapped behind a windscreen
dimming like a living room light
turning down
down
down
out.

WE

You must work from home.
I must go to work.

We are called key
or essential workers.

To our two-year-old we
are the swing social distancing

keeps her from. *Whee!*
she says, full of fun,

her hands in our hands:
she swings between us—

a metronome,
keeping our hearts in time.

# VITAL ORGANS

*ICU, Easter, 2020*

An outsider looking in might imagine
they were seeing the interior of a spaceship;
ventilators, dialysis machines, monitors
surrounded a station full of computers,
and strange-looking creatures
indistinguishable from one another.

In gowns, masks, goggles and gloves
with only a scribble like a tattoo above
the heart to tell who was who and what part
they played in a war against an invisible enemy
on a battlefield set up to monitor and measure
pulse rate, oxygen, blood pressure, temperature.

They moved around proned bodies
as if they themselves were one body.
Seven surrounded a bed;
three down either flank, one at the head
like a Captain turning a wheel
while talking a crew through a manoeuvre.

One dropped an Actichlor tablet into a bucket
and screwed a mop-head to a pole like a bayonet.
Another wheeled a dirty-linen hamper.
One did obs. Two made up drugs.
Another set up a trolley for intubation.
One spoke to a visitor via Zoom.

An insider looking in wouldn't know a porter
from a doctor, a domestic from a nurse.
Amid machines bleeping and flashing,
staff in aprons and gowns like layers of skin
worked as vital organs: each had a function:
a job to do so other jobs could be done.

VISITOR

Twenty miles from her bed,
iPad on knees, he watches
the face of his Mum.

A cord connected them
as this tube in her mouth
now hooks her to a machine

like a fishing line
he'd reel her home on
if he could pull her through.

## THE BIG MAN

*GOAT A LIGHT, BIG MAN?*
A bigger man than myself
shouted as I left the hospital.

*Dinnae smoke,* I telt him,
feeling my lips brush material
muzzling me, while

he coughed up phlegm
and gobbed a few inches from
a big NO SMOKING sign.

# PERSPECTIVE

> I worked as an orderly at the hospital
> without medicine and water...
> —Anna Świrszczyńska

After a third twelve-hour nightshift
the skin on my nose broke down.
I had to peel the fit-tested mask
blood-glued to the bone
as a dayshift colleague looked on
and squirmed away.

One thing you learn in ICU:
life can always be worse.
Looking in the mirror,
I could see things as they were.
I was no Anna Świr
in Warsaw, or Trakl in Grodeck.

Gruesome pictures of their
makeshift hospitals lived on
in poems beyond my blackened eyes
and sallow sleep-deprived skin,
and a nose opened up
like it had been punched in.

BABY DOLL

At two-and-a-half, Rosie is oblivious
to all but the baby doll in its pram,
though she stops every so often
when something snags her attention,

then moves on, as we must.
Sometimes she moves so fast
she falls. One time, hugging her close,
an elbow sliced the scab from my nose.

The sting went off like an alarm,
waking me to the pressure from
the mask that protects me at work.
And then I was standing in the dark

of our bedroom, 3 a.m.,
fumbling among bookshelves I mistook
for racks of PPE.
I was only going to the toilet

yet anxiously grasping for a mask.
But Rosie was over her fall
and bored with all
this hanging around in the head.

*Come on, Daddy!* she said.
And, like a child, I followed her lead.
It's all about the baby in the pram.
We can't stop now. We must go on.

## THE TAXI DRIVER EXPLAINS

*Men are bettir drivers hen,*
*specially in the snaw.*
*What's wi aw the empty wards then?*
*You're a nurse, where's the flu went?*
*No wearin a mask against the law?*

*Shite! Aw they statistics are bent.*
*Dinnae believe the media hen.*
*Vaccine? Probably grow anithir heid!*
*Madness hus buried this country like snaw.*
*Lockdoon's like bein deid.*

She'd felt his gaze dip her head-to-toe
and back again, and his hello
had been a dirty grin as she took in
his age and BMI and how he looked
just like all those other men.

Now the meter was rising
like a body count
as his tongue flapped on;
an auld tattered flag stirred by hot air.
*It jist kills auld fowk...*

When they got there she paid the fare,
slammed the door hard
and tossed words over her shoulder
soft as good luck charms.
*Stay Safe. Take care.*

## DAY & NIGHT

That day we went puddle-hunting in our wellies.
Whenever we caught a good one, we jumped in
to see if it hid a big splash or a wee splash.

Back home I found Ticklies nesting in your oxters:
wee birdies who feed fledglings on toddler-giggles!
Then it was sleepy-time for you; work-time for me.

That night, in full PPE, I was sent for a body bag
and went behind curtains drawn on a man's last day.

## SINKING & SWIMMING

For weeks of walks during lockdown
we picked sticks and stones at random

and threw them into the burn,
day after day, again and again.

And you began to learn
how some go on, as others go down.

## OVERTIME

In his prime, Prine bagged songs
full of compassion wrapped in wit
like gifts he'd deliver to strangers.

Entering an intensive care unit
overwhelmed by the virus that
killed him, I hear among the hum

of machines, the beep of alarms,
Prine's words enveloped in tunes
like letters he delivers, overtime.

## APRIL MORNING, 2020

For years half-a-dozen people
stood with me at this bus stop.
Now I stand alone with Prine
in my head. Next to no traffic
on a major road into Scotland's
largest city. Signs over the M80:

STAY HOME
PROTECT THE NHS
SAVE LIVES

Rain streaking the pane could be
music frequencies, sound waves
monitoring notes recorded before
I was born. I watch them
erased by wind as a dead man
sings into me, a reviving breath.

# THE RIG

*To my Dad in the hospital, Nov 2020*

Our caravan creaks in the wind
though the howling is drowned
in a hail of nails hammering
a thin skin of aluminium
sheltering us from the storm.

I think of the rigs you were on
in Shetland and Morecambe:
Fife Crusoe among the elements.
*No man is an island*—John Donne.
But you are the rig you worked on.

So deep in an ocean of your own,
so solid a foundation, unlike the caravan
I lie awake in now, thinking of you:
a man of few words, most would agree.
You always came home from sea.

## HEADS TURNING

The conspiracist shouting *HOAX!*
didn't believe in social distancing
so the porter walked up to him
and smashed his teeth in.

Left him sitting on a drain
as he'd left so many in the morgue,
though this one got up again.
*Did ye see what he done?*

No one saw a thing
that happened in front of them.
Heads turn from reality
for reasons of their own.

## THE LITTER-A-CHEWER

On a walk through the woods
Rosie found a glove and mask
hanging like fruit from a tree
and I recycled them into a story
about a strange-looking creature
with a book-shaped face
and teeth like sharp-edged paper.

The Litter-a-chewer turns rubbish
into manure and plants words
like seeds deep in the woods,
then regurgitates what it sows
into stories about huge-germs,
as it calls humans, and blows
fables into ears as it goes.

## SHIELDING

*What's that?* you asked,
hands on knees, face inches
from a shell.

*A snail,* I said.
It was still as us all
these last few weeks,

while the clock ticked on
gentle as a current eroding stone.
*It's shielding.*

I tasted the word as one
I hadn't tried before our home
became a shell for your Mum

to work in and shelter from
germs blowing through weeks
of days flowing one into the other.

We were gentle,
carrying the snail, and careful,
as we placed it in a garden.

Then we moved on,
not bothering to look down
at whatever wee thing

might drown in our tread.
We had to look ahead.
So we did.

## ROCKPOOLING

We poked in the shallows of pools
and picked up pebbles and shells.

A dead crab in the sand
turned into a creature fastened

to my face. It fed on my breath
until a small hand tugged my hand;

a soft bite of fingers, a gentle pull,
warm and vulnerable in a shell

of knuckles too open to form a fist.
I felt a jolt, and resurfaced.

## IT MIGHT NIVVER HAPPEN

(Three days after 'Freedom Day')

Men are drinking, singing, stamping
up the back of a jam-packed bus.
A mouth catches her attention
in a second's glance:
lips ripped apart by laughter,
sealed by a grin.

The face of a patient she helped un-prone
hours before sits with her:
mouth and chin bloody and torn
from tapes keeping the et tube in,
eyes swollen shut from being
in the same position eighteen hours.

A breeze wafts wet lashes.
A shoulder bumps her arm.
*Awright darlin?*
Beer-breath warms her skin.
*Cheer up hen!*
*It might nivver happen!*

'He had dreamt that the entire world had fallen victim
to some strange, unheard of and unprecedented plague
that was spreading from the depths of Asia into Europe...
never, never had they believed so unswervingly in the
correctness of their judgements, their scientific deductions,
their moral convictions and beliefs...each person thought
  that he alone possessed the truth.'
            —Fyodor Dostoyevksy, *Crime and Punishment*, 1866

The wall is full of self-care posters:
*Are you worried about Covid-19?*
Booklets spread across tables have titles:
*Depression; Anxiety; Stress; Anger.*
A number for a psychologist is pinned
by a window overlooking the Necropolis.
Glass frames a statue of John Knox.

Before he rose up to smash idolatry,
Knox was a slave in a galley.
Now his effigy glares at Glasgow Cathedral,
one of the few places of Catholic worship
the Reformation failed to smash up.
Across from the window, a television
frames activists tipping a statue into a harbour.

For weeks that screen has been a mirror
reflecting what's been going on in here
in ICUs, in cities across the country,
in countries across the world.
Now scenes unfold of statues toppling
like dominoes falling one into the other,
city to city, one country to the next.

I look at Knox and hear the knocks
of knuckles rapping through history;

fists ripping up one story for another
as my own tighten and whiten
into the hard skulls of men
capable of destruction and compassion:
palms opening out, knuckles closing in.

## AFTERTASTE

Covid comes up every so often
though much is a blank or a blur
or something sour in a cup
that when you swallow you wear
the aftertaste in a grimace.

Drop a detail on the floor
and like a match tossed to straw
dark corners are lit on what we saw:
how sick the patients were!
Would there be enough ventilators?

Were we safe? Anxious yelling
*don't come near me* as you ran
for a shower, clothes stuffed
into a dissolvable bag you'd ram
into the machine on a high wash.

Sleeping in separate rooms:
*what if I take it home?*
Neighbours applauding.
Signs in windows:
PROTECT THE NHS; rainbows.

Gallows humour to cope:
the windowless basement theatre-
turned-ICU—The Dungeon.
How loss of taste was a sign;
'partygate' hard to swallow.

*What keeps me awake at night*
*is chased away by the light*

*of a wee girl bouncing,*
*and a big smile announcing*

*the dark gone away!*
*The dark gone away!*

## THE COST OF LIVING

Here in Condorrat the nursery is shut
so adults with rosettes pinned to their hearts
can persuade us where to pin our hopes.

How to explain voting to you, aged four?
'What party would you vote for?'
'A birthday party; with balloons.'
'I think the balloon already has a party.'

Still, it's our duty to vote. I spell
D.U.T.Y and she becomes a character
in a story we take turns to tell.

Later, you yell *FASTER* on a swing
as 'Heat or eat' headlines bemoan
the cost of living on a mobile phone
I bury in a pocket so I can push you on.

NOTES

*Arrivals & Departures*

'Griffith'

Emile Griffith (1938–2013) was an undisputed world boxing champion
in three weight divisions. In 1962 his opponent Benny Paret died after
Griffith knocked him out in a world title fight broadcast live on TV.
Griffith was rumoured to be gay at the time. He would later come out
as bisexual.

'The Sleeping Giant'

Ramsay Mackay was born in Scotland in 1945 and moved to South
Africa in 1953. From 1966 to 1970 he was a member of the South
African prog-rock band Freedom's Children. He released a solo album,
*Suburbs Of Ur* in 1982. A few months before he died, I was surprised
and delighted to be reacquainted with Ramsay via Facebook. Much
of Ramsay's music is available on YouTube, including his late career
musical project with Henry Dennis, The Fumes of Mars.

'Brett's Jukebox Kitchen'

Brett Evans, poet and co-founder/co-editor of the poetry and prose
journal *Prole*, lives in North Wales. He doesn't have a cookery/poetry/
music TV show, but if he did I'd watch the telly more often.

'Comrade'

This poem is based on secondhand memories of a friend of my Dey
(Granddad,) a regular in the Kelty Ex-Serviceman's Club. I always
loved the irony, humour and affection in his nickname as much as I
disliked (while understanding the emotion fuelling it) Nye Bevan's
dehumanizing of the Tories: 'As far as I am concerned they are lower
than vermin.'

'Banter'

The Hielanman's Umbrella is the Glaswegian nickname for the glass-walled railway bridge of Glasgow Central station across Argyle Street. During the second phase of the Highland Clearances in the 19th century around 30,000 Gaelic-speaking displaced highlanders came to Glasgow to find work. They would often use the railway bridge as a meeting place and shelter.

'The Whys'

833 suicides were registered in Scotland in 2019: 620 males, 213 females. According to Public Health Scotland, 'There is a known link between deprivation and suicide. The probable suicide rate in the period 2016–2020 was three-and-a-half times higher in the most deprived areas compared to the least deprived areas.'

'Remembrance Service, 1936'

'The Soldier' refers to the Kelty War Memorial by sculptor William Birnie Rhind.

'Hope Street, 2017'

'The Flyting of MacDiarmid and Henderson' refers to a public debate conducted during the 1960s between Hugh MacDiarmid (1892–1978), Hamish Henderson (1919–2002) and other poets and academics regarding the merits and differences between folk song and art poetry.

The lines about poets fighting in a captain's tower allude to 'Desolation Row' (1966) by Bob Dylan.

In 2017 some tabloids referred to then Prime Minister Theresa May as 'Mayhem.'

'January Morning, 2020'

Nye Bevan (1897–1960,) the architect of the NHS, educated himself via the Tredegar Workmen's Institute Library in South Wales.

John Baird (1790–1820) was a weaver from Condorrat, North Lanarkshire, who became a revolutionary commander in the 1820 uprising. Seen today by many as a martyr for universal suffrage, he was hanged and beheaded as a traitor at Stirling in 1820. Weavers in Scotland at that time were well known for their literacy.

Due to austerity cuts implemented in 2010 almost 800 libraries had closed by December 2019.

The iconic social reformer and abolitionist Frederick Douglass (1818–1895) called James McCune Smith (1813–1865) the most important influence in his life. I'd no idea who Smith was until I started working in Glasgow Royal Infirmary and found myself walking by a large framed portrait before and after every shift.

'The Grey Zone' is a chapter in Primo Levi's book, *The Drowned and the Saved* (1986).


'*Days & Nights*'

Most of these poems are based on my personal experience working as an Auxiliary Nurse in Intensive Care during the pandemic. In the interests of confidentiality I never mention specific details in regard to patients: scenes depicted in poems like 'Visitor' were sadly witnessed many times and are not based on individuals. All views expressed are my private views and do not represent those of NHS Greater Glasgow and Clyde. Exceptions to this are the character-based poems expressing anti-vaxx or Covid-denying views. These are fictional composites of people I witnessed or read about outside of work. I have included them to provide some variation in tone and perspective and to provide a contrast to my own experience.

'Vital Organs'

Proning: the placement of patients into a prone position so they are
lying on their stomach. Traditionally used in the treatment of patients
in intensive care with acute respiratory distress syndrome to improve
their breathing, the procedure requires sedated intubated patients
be lifted and turned and usually takes six or seven members of staff
to achieve safely. Proning is rarely used but during the first wave of
the pandemic proning teams would move from bed to bed, patient to
patient. At the time of writing videos are available on YouTube showing
staff in full PPE practising proning.

'Perspective'

The poet Anna Świrszczyńska (1909–1984) was a military nurse in
the Polish Resistance during the Warsaw Uprising against the Nazis in
1944. Her poetry collection *Building the Barricade* (1974) documents
her experiences working in makeshift hospitals lacking bandages and
medicine in a city bombed day and night by German planes and tanks.
'Although no one forced us, we built the barricade, under fire,' Świr
wrote of those fighting to survive in a city deprived of water, electricity,
gas, food supplies and with a sewage system that didn't function
properly and the full force of a well-equipped German army instructed
by Himmler that 'Warsaw must be razed to the ground, in order to serve
as a deterring example for the whole of Europe.'

The poet and pharmacist Georg Trakl (1887–1914) was a Dispensing
Officer in the Medical Corps of the Austrian Army at the battle of
Grodeck where he found himself in charge of a barn full of ninety
severely wounded soldiers and no supplies. He committed suicide in
a psychiatric ward later that year.

'Overtime'

The American singer-songwriter John Prine (1946–2020) died from
complications of Covid-19. He wrote his early songs while working as a
postman. His music kept me company commuting to work during the
first wave of the pandemic.

'The Rig'

Alexander Selkirk (1676–1721), the inspiration for Daniel Defoe's novel, *Robinson Crusoe*, came from Lower Largo in Fife.

No man is an Iland, intire of itselfe; every man
is a peece of the Continent, a part of the maine;

From: MEDITATION XVII,
*Devotions upon Emergent Occasions* by John Donne, 1624.

My Dad worked offshore as an electrician most of his working life. He was admitted to hospital for an emergency procedure in Nov 2020, spent a night in intensive care, and caught Covid in a ward. He came home.


'Heads Turning'

I wrote this poem after seeing footage of Covid deniers protesting outside St Thomas's hospital, London, on New Year's Eve, 2020. I don't recall hearing of any violent assaults like the one in the poem but remember reflecting on the mounting tension and fearing what might lie ahead.


'It Might Nivver Happen'

19th July 2021 was declared Freedom Day in England. The British Medical Association regarded this as a 'gamble.' In Scotland, at this time, I was increasingly seeing people in greater numbers without masks on public transport, including, on a few occasions, beer-drinking men.

Et tube: endotracheal tube, a flexible tube through the nose or, more commonly, the mouth into the trachea, or windpipe, to help a patient breathe.

'Windows & Mirrors'

John Knox (1514–1572) was the leader of the Protestant Reformation in Scotland. He spent nineteen months enslaved in a French galley where he was chained to a bench and forced to row. An advocate of violent revolution, Knox preached against Catholic idolatry. His sermons incited riots and vandalism.

A statue of 17th-century slave trader Edward Colston (1636–1721) was toppled during a Black Lives Matter protest in Bristol on the 7th June, 2020, in the wake of George Floyd's murder by the police in Minneapolis. Other monuments and memorials symbolizing colonial history were vandalized or removed at this time, mainly in the United States but also in several other countries.

'Aftertaste'

'Partygate' was a political scandal during the pandemic where members of the Conservative government, including the Prime Minister Boris Johnson, broke the law by hosting parties while the rest of the country were expected to obey the government's lockdown restriction policy in the interest of public safety.

## Acknowledgements

Thanks are due to the editors of the following publications where several of these poems first appeared:

*Atrium, Bad Lilies, The Dark Horse, Gutter, Honest Ulsterman, London Grip, Northwords Now, Stand, Poetry Birmingham Literary Journal, Poets' Republic, Poetry Scotland, Wild Court.*

I am also grateful to Gregor Addison and Gerry Cambridge for their feedback on early versions of these poems, to Andrew Neilson for his advice on an early version of the typescript, to Colin Will for editing it, and to Gerry Cambridge for typesetting, designing and turning it into the book it is. And finally to my publisher Sheila Wakefield, Founder and Editor at Red Squirrel Press without whom this book would not be in your hands right now.

This book is set in Foundry Wilson, a redrawing of a 1760 font from Scottish type founder Alexander Wilson (1714–1786), a polymath who from 1760 to 1786 was the University of Glasgow's first Regius Professor of Astronomy. Many of Wilson's typefaces were produced exclusively for the Foulis brothers' classics published by Glasgow University Press. Like its nominal descendant, the author of *Vital Signs,* Foundry Wilson is highly distinctive and robust; a serif typeface which functions excellently in a digital environment.